Robin Hood's

fame has reached all corners of the Earth. In England he is regarded as the most popular bandit hero of all time. He has been a household name for at least six hundred years.

Everyone has a soft spot for the gallant character who tradition has it robbed the rich to feed the poor, who waged war against corruption, tyranny and injustice yet was loyal to his monarch, god-fearing and courteous. The vision of Robin and his merry band living and performing their many deeds in the greenwoods is stamped on the imagination of their admirers.

No one knows for certain if Robin ever really lived but it could be that the stories were founded on a real person who lived over six hundred years ago. After all there is no smoke without fire! Robin may appear in the tales to be somewhat larger than life – but why not? Other famous heroes, such as King Arthur and St. George in England, William Tell in Switzerland, Ned Kelly in Australia, El Cid in Spain and many of the great American cowboys have similarly passed into legend.

The Tales of Robin Hood

The Quest for Robin Hood

Robin was not only a celebrity, but also a character of mystery. Not only have people impersonated him, but they have also assumed his name. Other people have searched for him through tons of documents. Some have claimed to have tracked him down. Others even have relied on conjecture and elaborated on fiction. Early ballad stories are of little help in finding him. There is little about him and his origins. He had acquired a renown for his prowess in the martial arts: the long bow, the sword and the staff. He is referred to as a yeoman which implies that he was an officer or higher servant in a noble or gentry household, or was a farmer holding land. The farming yeomen were a new and rising class who were to play an important role in the English economy during the 1400's and 1500's. Moreover, it is implied in the Geste that Robin had been outlawed but no reason is given. Nothing of the age in which he lived is recounted apart from a small clue in the Geste referring to Edward "our comely King." This King could possibly by Edward II. In the Geste there is a description of Robin's encounter with the King which resembles a chronicler's actual account of Edward II's progress to Nottingham in 1323. On the other hand, it could be a reference to either Edward I or Edward III. Between them, the three Edwards reigned for 105 years, from 1272 to 1377. Place names in the early ballads can be clearly identified today. Some of the action took place in the area around Barnsdale in Yorkshire and in and around Sherwood Forest in Nottinghamshire. According to the ballad story, Robin died at Kirk Lees which is about 20 miles as the crow flies north-west from Barnsdale.

Robin Hood and the Historians

By the 1400's, there was a conscious attempt to discover Robin Hood. The first three historians to mention Robin were Scotsmen. Andrew of Wyntoun who wrote his "Metrical Chronicle" in about 1420 assigns Robin and Little John to Barnsdale in Yorkshire and Inglewood in Cumberland round about the year 1283. The second, Walter Bower who revised Fordun's "Scotichronicon" in about 1450 added a passage mentioning Robin roaming around the countryside in the years after Simon de Montfort's revolt in about 1266. The third Scot, John Major who published his History of Great Britain in 1521 writes "About the time of King Richard I, according to my estimate the famous English robber Robert Hood and Little John were lurking in their woods, preying on the goods of the wealthy."

None of the three give any hint of the sources they used. Probably they relied entirely on various stories that were being hawked around. Clearly they cannot all have been right – Major's Robin living in about 1188 would have been well over one hundred years of age if he was the same Robin as the one mentioned by Wyntoun and Bower who lived in the late 1200's!

King Edward III (1327-1377) about 1355, St. Stephen's Chapel, Palace of Westminster. At the end of his reign, William Langland wrote a "Vision of Piers Plowman" which has the earliest known reference to Robin Hood.

Robin Hood Earl of Huntingdon

There must have been stories circulating round about 1500 which have now been lost. John Leland writing in the early 1500's stated that Robin was buried at Kirk Lees. A contemporary gave Robin's birth place as Locksley. One generally held to be true at the time was that Robin lived the reign of Richard I and was the rightful Earl of Huntingdon. He had thus been upgraded from yeoman to Earl! It was a theme that was to be taken up later by a distinguished antiquarian William Stukeley who in 1746 published an account of Robin. In it he claimed that Robin lived in the reign of Henry III, was the rightful Earl of Huntingdon and was also none other than Robert Fitzooth, Lord of the manor of Loxley in Warwickshire with a family tree that stretched back to one of William the Conqueror's barons. Thomas Gale, Dean of York, 1697-1702, recorded that Robin died on 24 Kalends of December 1247. Sadly there is no such date according to the Roman calendar! Alas all these claims are totally bogus and there is not a shred of evidence to support any of them. Nevertheless Stukeley's allegations have been reiterated by many writers since then as if they were gospel truths. Another source of interest has been Robin's supposed grave at Kirk Lees. Several grave stones have been erected over the centuries. One standing in the 1600's gave an actual date for Robin's death – 4 December 1198. This was a fake probably erected and inscribed sometime about 1600. The grave was excavated in 1784 but unfortunately no remains were found.

Manuscripts and Robin Hood

In the 1800's and 1900's the historian instead of relying on hearsay and an over vivid imagination as his predecessors had done, started the lengthy task of sifting through documents in his search for Robin. One, Joseph Hunter claimed in 1852 to have found the genuine Robin Hood – Robert Hood, mentioned in Edward II's household accounts in 1324 as a valet, and also between 1316 and 1317 he found Robert Hood and his wife Matilda in the Court Rolls of the Manor of Wakefield. But in fact Hunter could not find proof that these two Roberts were the same person or that they were outlaws. He did surmise that Robin was a supporter of the rebellious Earl of Lancaster but was later pardoned by the King.

An antiquarian, J. W. Walker writing in 1944 and 1952, attempted to uphold Hunter's ideas but without any new factual basis. Other historians have examined the Wakefield Court Rolls for further evidence, and have concluded that in the early 1300's, there were several different Hoods including at least two Roberts living at the same time. Another candidate, who is the only Robert Hood later called Hobbehod, known to have been an outlaw, was summoned in 1225 and 1226 to appear before the assizes in York but apparently he fled and was henceforth referred to as a fugitive or an outlaw. Nothing more was heard of him. Yet another Robin Hood, this time at Rockingham in Northamptonshire, was accused of a forest offence in 1354. Not only was Hood a fairly common surname in England, but also Robert or Robin was a popular Christian name. Professor James Holt writing in 1960 and in 1982, looked for other evidence by examining the unusual and rare surname of "Robynhod," suggesting that it might have been linked with the famous outlaw. A Gilbert Robynhod was living in Sussex in 1296. Two different Robert Robynhods lived in London between 1294 and 1332. One gave his name to a London inn – the "Hostil Robin Hood." Holt finds a curious link between Sussex and the Barnsdale area in Yorkshire. Gilbert Robynhod tenanted land at Lewes in Sussex off Thomas, Earl of Lancaster who also held land at Wakefield and had married the heiress of the Honour of Pontefract in which Barnsdale lay. A strange coincidence! Professor Holt also thinks that as the stories of Robin Hood were so well founded by 1377, the legendary outlaw, if he existed at all, must have done so some considerable time before – probably in the 1200's. So far, Robin has eluded capture.

the birth of the legends

& the Robin Hood stories

¶ Here begynneth a gest of Robyn Hode

The tales of Robin were being recounted over six hundred years ago. In those days when few people could read or write rarely were such stories written down. Traditionally wandering minstrels roamed the countryside telling or singing of the deeds of great heroes and events of the past – in fact and fiction. Audiences always wanted to hear old familiar stories but often in a new and exciting guise. So the tales grew and changed as the years passed by. History and legend became hopelessly confused. For instance, the adventures and exploits of many bandits, outlaws and others were joined together with contemporary beliefs and attitudes. Out of such a medley emerged the stories of Robin Hood and his merry men. Many stories must have perished but fortunately some have survived.

The earliest known mention of Robin is in William Langland's famous poem – "The vision of William concerning Piers Plowman." written down in about 1377 where the rhymes of Robin Hood are spoken of.

"I do not know my paternoster perfectly as the priest sings it.
But I know rhymes of Robin Hood and Randolph, earl of Chester."

Robin Hood in Print

The tantalising glimpse in Piers Plowman places Robin Hood fairly and squarely on the map as a figure to be reckoned with. Soon afterwards other references appear but the earliest story of his exploits to survive was written down on parchment in about 1450. The setting up in London of the printing press by William Caxton in 1477 made it possible for more and cheaper books to be produced. Robin appears in print sometime between 1500 and 1530 when the most popular of all the ballads "A Geste of Robyn Hode" was published. Other stories followed and new variations were added to the old themes. In the 1500's and 1600's a whole host of such stories were printed such as "Robin Hood and Guy of Gisborne," "Robin Hood and the Monk," "Robin Hood and the Potter," "Robin Hood's Death," "The Jolly Pinder of Wakefield," "Robin Hood and the Butcher," "Robin Hood and the Curtal Friar," "Robin Hood and Little John," "Robin Hood and Allan A Dale," "Robin Hood and Maid Marian." In most of them the action takes place in and around Barnsdale in South Yorkshire, in York and in Nottingham and Sherwood Forest.

9

A Geste of Robyn Hode

The Geste is the best known of the tales. Manuscript accounts survive from the late 1400's and the first printed versions came in the early 1500's. In the original version of this ballad three different tales are told —

Robin Hood and the Knight,
Little John and the Sheriff of Nottingham, and
The King and Robin Hood.

A mery geste of
Robyn Hoode and of hys lyfe, wyth a newe playe for to be played in Maye games very plesaunte and full of pastyme.
](•••)[

A Geste of Robyn Hode

Robin Hood and the Knight

IN the first of these "Robin Hood and the Knight," the setting is in Barnsdale forest where Robin and his boon companions Little John, Scarlet and Much the Miller's Son are looking for adventure Robin wants to entertain a guest for dinner, so the gang set out in search for one. They are told to "harm no husbande that tilleth with his ploughe" nor a good yeoman or a knight or a squire that "wol be a gode felawe," but rather to entice a member of the clergy or even the Sheriff of Nottingham whom they are to "beat and bind." The gang come across a down at heel knight who accepts their invitation to dine with their master. He is courteously received by Robin but when the meal is over, is unable to pay for it as is expected by the outlaws' custom. He confesses he has only ten shillings (50p) which when checked is found to be correct by Little John. Robin will not accept a penny but requests the knight to tell his story, which is one of misfortune. His son has killed a Lancashire knight and his squire and now the knight has to buy his son's freedom. The knight's lands have been pledged for the sum of £400 to the Abbot of St. Mary's, York. As he has no money he cannot repay the loan to he stands to lose his lands. Robin lends him the money, and the knight pledges repayment in the name of the Virgin Mary. Robin who is very religious and especially devoted to the Virgin Mary accepts this. The knight is also presented with new clothes, a horse, boots and spurs and is to be accompanied by Little John acting as his squire on the journey to York. The knight arrives dressed in his old shabby clothes and feigns inability to repay the loan. The jubilant abbot hoping to confiscate the knight's land refuses to grant any reprieve. But much to his surprise and annoyance the knight disdainfully counts out £400 and then leaves to return home to Wyresdale in Lancashire where he starts raising the money he owes to Robin. Back in Barnsdale forest Robin asks Little John and the others to go out in search of another "paying guest." They come across a monk, none other than the High Cellerar from St. Mary's Abbey, York journeying to London accompanied by a retinue of 52 men. These are put to flight by the outlaws and the cellerar is captured and taken back to Robin's camp. After the meal payment is requested but the cellerar claims to have only 20 marks, but on examination the untruthful monk has £800 which Robin keeps, allowing his captive to go free. The knight arrives to repay the money but Robin will not take it, saying that the Virgin Mary has with the assistance of the cellerar already repaid the debt. Robin accepts the gift of 100 bows and arrows from him and then gives him half of the cellerar's money as a generous bonus. The companions and the knight give thanks to the Virgin Mary for their good fortune and then take their leave of each other.

Robin Hood and the Knight, from Howard Pyle's "Merry Adventures of Robin Hood."

Little·John·overcomes·Eric·o'·Lincoln

12

A Geste of Robyn Hode

Little John and the Sheriff of Nottingham

THE second story of the Geste is about "Little John and the Sheriff of Nottingham." The action takes place in and around Nottingham. Little John excels at an archery contest and makes such an impression on the sheriff, that the sheriff hires him for a year, although Little John explains that he is already serving a courteous knight. Little John, who now changes his name to Reynold Greenleaf, is determined to serve the sheriff badly. The sheriff goes out hunting leaving Little John behind him still in bed. Little John after quarrelling with the sheriff's butler, then fights with the cook who puts up such impressive resistance that Little John persuades him to join the outlaws in the forest and the two go off and join forces with Robin Hood. Little John then sets out and finding the sheriff promises to show him a "ryght fayre harte" with a herd of seven score of deer. But instead the unsuspecting sheriff is brought to Robin Hood.

Humiliated, the sheriff is then forced to eat a meal off his very own silver. He is stripped of his fine apparel and obliged to dress as an outlaw in Lincoln green. To crown it all, he has to spend the night on the ground. Next morning, aching in every limb he promises in exchange for his freedom to leave the outlaws unmolested. Some time later, he is determined to get his revenge and organises an archery contest at which Robin, Little John, Scarlet, Much the Miller and two new companions Gilbert of the White Hand and Reynold, all excel. Robin wins the prize – a gold and silver arrow – but then is treacherously set upon by the sheriff and his men who also seriously wound Little John. Little John entreats Robin to kill him so that he will not fall alive into the sheriff's hands, but the two make their way to the castle of Sir Richard. This Sir Richard turns out to be the same knight to whom Robin lent the money. King Edward, informed by the sheriff of the outlaws' deeds, is coming to punish them in person. In the meantime, the sheriff captures Sir Richard who is out hawking in the forest and imprisons him in Nottingham where the outlaws kill the sheriff and release Sir Richard. The companions all return to the forest to await the king's pardon.

THE KING PARDONS ROBYN

A GESTE OF ROBYN HODE

Left. *The King pardons Robin. From "The Legend of Robyn Hode and Mery Scherewode."*

Centre. *The King and Robin Hood. From "The Legend of Robyn Hode and Mery Scherewode."*

Right. *A medieval English King. Stained glass from "The Legend of Robyn Hode and Mery Scherewode."*

14

The KING and Robin Hood

THE king enraged by the deeds of Robin, his companions and Sir Richard, arrives in Nottingham thirsting for revenge. Robin is nowhere to be found but eventually an old forester tells the king of Robin's abode. The king and five knights disguised as an an abbot and monks ride into the forest and are waylaid by Robin and his gang.

The king still in disguise confesses that life at court is so expensive that he has only £40 left. This Robin takes, giving half to his companions and the other half back to his captive who then tells Robin he has a message from the king bidding Robin to go to Nottingham. This gives Robin the chance to declare his unanswering loyalty to his monarch. After a feast of venison, white bread, red wine and brown ale, they all join in an archery contest at which Robin excels. Eventually, however, he misses the target and as a penalty is given an almighty blow by the disguised king, whom Robin immediately recognises because of his enormous strength. Robin, his companions and Sir Richard all kneel down and pay homage to the king, who readily pardons them all. The king then returns to Nottingham and decides to play a prank on the citizens. He has already bought Lincoln green cloth from Robin and uses it to dress himself and his courtiers up as outlaws. The citizens are panic stricken and at first believe the king has been killed but he is recognised and the whole town rejoices. Robin and his companions accept the king's invitation to live at court.

"Robyn toke the kynges hors,
Hastely in that stede,
And sayd' Syr abbot, by your leve,
A whyle ye must abyde.

We be yemen of the foreste,
Under the grene wode tre;
We lyve by our kynges dere,
Other shyft have not we,

And ye have chyches and tentes both,
And gold full grete plente,
Gyve us some of your spendynge,
For sayte charyte."

Inevitably, they grow weary of court life and one by one drift back to the forest until only Robin, Little John, and Will Scarlet are left. Robin wants to go back to Barnsdale and the Chapel which he has built there. The king grants him leave of absence for one week only, but once Robin is back in the greenwood he blows his horn and seven score yeomen flock to him. He decides to risk the king's wrath and stay in his old haunts away from court. There Robin lives for another twenty two years, until he falls ill and goes to Kirk Lees Priory for treatment and to be bled. His kinswoman, the Prioress of Kirk Lees and her lover Sir Roger of Doncaster take advantage of him and treacherously kill him.

A manuscript copy dated from about 1450 is the first evidence of this ballad. Praised by many as the finest of the early tales it was not printed until 1806. Because some verses of the ballad have been lost it is not clear how the story develops.

Robin Hood and the Monk

THE story opens in leafy Sherwood on a May morning with sun shining and the birds singing. Little John is enjoying it all, but not so Robin Hood who regrets that he has not been to Church for a fortnight. He decides to make amends and goes to Nottingham accompanied only by Little John. On the way they shoot for pennies and Little John wins five shillings from Robin who is so angry that he quarrels bitterly with Little John. They part company – Little John returning to the forest while Robin goes on to Nottingham to say his prayers at St. Mary's. He is recognised by a monk who betrays him to the sheriff. All the gates of the town are closed and with a large body of men the sheriff attacks Robin who now regrets quarrelling with Little John whose help he desperately needs. He defends himself bravely but at last breaks his sword on the sheriff's thick skull. Eventually Little John and the rest of the gang have

news of Robin's capture. They are despondent but only Little John has hope claiming that because Robin has such faith in the Virgin Mary she will save him. The gang already know that the monk who betrayed Robin is travelling to the king with letters about Robin's capture. Little John and Much, after catching up with the monk, brutally murder him and take the letters themselves to the king. The monarch is delighted at Robin's capture and sends the outlaws back to Nottingham with a message that Robin is to be brought to court alive. Little John explains the disappearance of the monk to the sheriff by saying that the king has made him Abbot of Westminster. Little John and Much then rescue Robin at night while the sheriff is drunk. Robin and Little John are reconciled and return to the forest, but the king is angry because he has been fooled by Little John. Nevertheless, the monarch praises Little John's loyalty to his master Robin Hood.

Opposite. *The Archery Contest by Peter Dennis.*

A bag of money. From "The Legend of Robyn Hode and Mery Scherewode."

Left. *Corrupt and avaricious monks and priests were the favourite victims of Robin Hood and his band. From "The Legend of Robyn Hode and Mery Scherewode."*

17

Robin Hood and Guy of Gisborne

The first version of this popular ballad is in a manuscript dated about 1500. It is probably the most dramatic and also the most violent of the early stories but was not printed until 1765.

ET in Barnsdale, Robin has had a dream of being tied up and beaten by two young yeomen. Robin and Little John go out to find these two characters. They meet a well armed man leaning against a tree, but quarrel over who shall attack him. Little John goes back to Barnsdale where the rest of the merry men have been routed by the sheriff and his men. Little John breaks his bow while killing one of them and is taken prisoner and bound to a tree on which the sheriff assures him he will hang. Meanwhile Robin has met a stranger who says he is looking for Robin Hood. Unaware of each other's identity they challenge each other to an archery contest in which Robin displays his mastery. The stranger is amazed at the other's skill and asks his name. Robin tells him who he is and the stranger turns out to be Sir Guy of Gisborne. After a long drawn out sword fight Guy is killed and Robin cuts off his head which he mutilates so that it will not be recognisable and then sticks it on his bow. He then puts on Guy's clothes and throws his green coat over the body. The sheriff hearing the sound of Guy's horn joyfully calls out that Robin is slain. Robin still dressed as Guy goes to the sheriff who takes him to be Guy and grants his request that he may kill Little John. Robin of course goes out and frees Little John and gives him Guy's bow. Together they put the sheriff and his men to flight and Little John kills the fleeing sheriff. So ends the gruesome carnage.

Opposite. *Robin Hood in combat with Guy of Gisborne. From an original engraving by Bewick in Joseph Ritson's "Robin Hood."*

Left. *Illustration by Howard Pyle from his "Merry Adventures of Robin Hood."*

Above. *From an engraving in Pierce Egan's "Robin Hood and Little John."*

Of the several versions of this story which survive, the first is a printed broadsheet dating from about 1660. No doubt this was based on an earlier version which has been lost.

Robin Hood
and the
Curtal Friar

THE curtal (probably meaning short coated) friar is in popular imagination linked with Friar Tuck. Will Scarlet tells Robin of a curtal friar from Fountains Abbey who can shoot better than both Little John and Robin together. Robin vows neither to eat nor drink until he has met this man. The two of them meet on the banks of a stream while the rest of the merry men hide in the nearby ferns. Robin demands that the friar carry him across the stream. On the other bank, the friar threatens to kill Robin if he does not carry him back. This Robin does, but once again, he asks the friar to take him across. Without a word, the friar does as he is bid, but drops Robin in mid-stream. When both have swum to the bank, Robin draws his bow and shoots arrows at the friar which the friar repels with his buckler (a small shield). They fight from ten o'clock in the morning to four in the afternoon without result. When Robin blows his horn – the friar says he can blow it till his eyes drop out – fifty of Robin's yeomen appear. The friar retaliates by whistling, and then fifty of his dogs appear. He wants to match a dog against a man but Robin will not agree and instead makes his peace with the friar and invites him to join the outlaws.

Left. *Two illustrations by Howard Pyle from his "Merry Adventures of Robin Hood."*

Above. *The Friar carrying Robin Hood across the river. From an engraving by Bewick in Joseph Ritson's "Robin Hood."*

Above. *Friar Tuck by Peter Dennis.*

21

Robin Hood's death

There are many modern versions of this well known tale but the earliest surviving one is taken from a manuscript dated about 1760 which is believed to have been based on evidence that is now lost.

THE first part of the story is similar to that told in the Geste, but then new details are narrated. Roger of Doncaster becomes Red Roger. Robin is at Kirk Lees waiting to be bled. He summons Little John by three blasts on his horn. Robin who is mortally wounded by the wicked Roger is, nevertheless, still strong enough to smite off Roger's head with his sword. The dying Robin commands Little John to bear him up on his back and dig a grave, in which Robin is to be placed with his sword at his head, and at his side his bow, and his arrows at his feet.

Another version of Robin's death of slightly later date relates to the well known story of the shooting of the arrow.

Centre. *Robin shoots his last arrow, by Peter Dennis.*

Bottom left. *Robin's funeral, from an engraving by Bewick in Joseph Ritson's "Robin Hood."*

Bottom right. *The arrow marks the spot. From "The Legend of Robyn Hode and Mery Scherewode."*

Robin · ſhooteth · his · Laſt · Shaft :

H.P.

"I ne'er hurt fair maid in all my time,
    Not at my end shall it be;
But give me my bent bow in my hand,
    And my broad arrows I'll let flee.

And where this arrow is taken up,
    There shall my grave digged be,
With verdant sods most neatly put,
    Sweet as the greenwood trees."

ROBIN HOODS DEATH AND BURIAL

23

24

the Characters

Little John

From the earliest ballads Little John is depicted as Robin's right hand man and trustiest companion. Turbulent though their relationship is, Little John is loyally devoted to Robin as any liegeman is to his lord. Renowned for his strength and skill with the bow, Little John, it was claimed, was 7 feet tall. Controversy exists over his supposed place of burial. Tradition gives him three graves – one in Ireland where he was said to have been executed, another in Scotland and one at Hathersage in Derbyshire. In the last one, when opened in 1784, it was stated that a thigh bone of 29½ inches long – since lost – was found together with several pigs' bones.

Maid Marian

Beautiful, accomplished and feminine and yet often disguised as a boy, Maid Marian did not join Robin in legend until the 1500's. Traditionally she was part of the merry band from an earlier date and was portrayed in Tudor times as "a smurkynge wenche indeed . . . none of the coy dames." With Robin she became a leading figure in May Day festivities throughout the country – and so her fame grew.

Friar Tuck

The "Jolly" Friar probably made his first known appearance as one of Robin's men in a play performed in the 1470's. It was not until later that he became an indispensable member of Robin's band. He is the only historical outlaw, and was known as "frere Tuck", alias Robert Stafford, a Sussex chaplain, living in 1417 when he was chief of a gang of thieves and marauders. In the ballads he is the curtal friar who beat Robin in combat.

Will Scarlet

Better known as Will Scarlock or Scathelock, he appears in the earliest ballads as a trusty henchman of Robin and said to be his kinsman. He is a much more shadowy figure than Little John.

Allan A Dale

The minstrel who strummed his harp and sang the ballad songs did not join Robin until the 1600's. The story is that Robin helped this penniless lad to win the girl he loved from a rich old knight.

Others

Much the Miller's Son a stout and somewhat witless fellow, Gilbert of the White Hand and George a Green, The Pinder of Wakefield were also "valient men" in Robin's band.

Sir Richard of the Lee

Sir Richard who appears in the Geste may be an amalgamation of two historical characters. Firstly, there was a Sir Richard Foliot who not only held lands on the east side of Sherwood Forest but also near Wentbridge close to Barnsdale. Unlike the legendary Sir Richard, he unfortunately had to surrender his castle to the sheriff. Secondly, in the Geste, the knight returns home to Verysdale.

Could this possibly be Wryesdale in Lancashire in which the village of Lee is situated? Nearby there was to be found the family called La Legh and 20 miles east is Gisburn, linked with Guy of Gisborne.

The Sheriff

The villainous and wicked sheriff appears in the ballads as a figure beneath contempt whom no one can trust. He is lampooned and outwitted on every occasion. In the Middle Ages the sheriff was a very important and powerful figure. He was the king's representative in the counties and the boroughs for the maintenance of law and order and for the supervision of collecting taxes. Often, as well, he looked after the royal hunting forests with the power to punish poachers. His job made him unpopular, but to make matters worse he was often corrupt as well. Perhaps the sheriff in the ballads was based on the character of a real Sheriff of Nottingham.

Three historical candidates have been suggested. Firstly, Philip Mark was Sheriff of Nottinghamshire and Derbyshire from 1209 to 1224. Secondly, Brian De Lisle became Chief Forester of Nottinghamshire and Derbyshire from 1209 to 1217, Chief Justice of the Forest from 1221 to 1224 and Sheriff of Yorkshire in 1233/4. Thirdly, Eustace of Lowdham was Sheriff of Yorkshire from 1225 to 1226, and of Nottinghamshire 1232 to 1233 and also was a Forest Justice.

25

background to the ballad stories

The Audience

In the 1400's at a time when the earliest surviving ballads were circulating life no doubt for many people was hard but not totally bleak. The lord of the manor may have been harsh, taxation may have been heavy, but not all the time was spent working. There were many feast days and holidays and the evenings when there was time to sit by the fire in the great hall and listen to tales about the ancestors, legendary heroes, outlaws and the happenings in the past and to reflect on the times in which they lived. The Robin Hood ballads became something to which people could turn for relief. They embody a spirit of adventure extolling the martial arts and many ideas such as the dissatisfaction with the Church, not on religious grounds, but because of avarice and greed of the arch bishops, and particularly monks. The Church was already taking Robin seriously and was indignant at some of the anti-church sentiments expressed in the Geste. Several clerics remonstrated. One in about 1410 chastised those who "gou levir to heryn a tale or song robyn hode or of sum rubandry than to heryn messe or matynes." In spite of such strictures Robin's fame grew. Tyranny, injustice, corruption and oppressive forest law are also highlighted. Here the sheriff, who was the king's officer in charge of the local forests and an important official, is portrayed as the villain. He is lampooned, mocked, outwitted and shown to be ineffectual, which is perhaps an indication that forest law was in decline and that forests were much freer places than they had been in about 1200.

Nevertheless certain virtues were praised. Robin Hood, in spite of his attacks on the church for their avarice and greed, is devout and pious. His devotion to the Virgin Mary – the Mother of Christ – is exemplary and no doubt an indication of the importance of the role of religion in everyday life at the time. Robin is also a loyal subject of the king but

26

he steals the king's deer and has to be punished. It is not the king but rather the corrupt officialdom in the guise of the wicked sheriff that Robin is attacking. Once the king is reached, he is shown to be an entirely honourable, good and forgiving man who has unfortunately become alienated from his people by such creatures as corrupt sheriffs. No doubt this is an indication of how people at the time wanted to see their king. Charity is also commended even if it is in the form of an impoverished and wronged knight benefitting from the corrupt church. Moreover, the righting of wrongs is so often emphasised. There were many outlaws and brigands roaming the countryside and the towns in the late Middle Ages. Some even took the name of Robin Hood or were likened to him. For instance in 1439, Piers Venables, a Derbyshire criminal was accused of behaving like Robin Hood. Later in 1497 Rober Marchell from Wednesbury in Staffordshire was prosecuted in the name of Robin Hood – having led a group of more than 100 men to a riotous assembly at Willenhall. Much later in 1605, James I's famous Minister Sir Robert Cecil castigated Guy Fawkes and his associates as "Robin Hoods." Some brigands were simply referred to as "Robert's men."

The deeds of others very much resembled those recounted in the ballads. Roger Godberd who robbed, pillaged, plundered and murdered his way through the East Midlands and particularly Sherwood Forest between 1267 and 1272 was eventually captured by the King's Justicar, Reginald de Grey. In Derbyshire, the Coterels terrorised and murdered avaricious landowners. In Leicestershire the Folville brothers of Ashby Folville committed similar acts. They murdered Roger Bellars, a baron of the Exchequer in 1326, it is said in revenge for injustices he had done to them. Then in 1332 they kidnapped Sir Richard Willoughby, a justice of the King's Bench and held him to ransom, because of supposed injustices. One of the brothers, Richard, murdered a pursuer in self defence, but as was Robin Hood, they were all pardoned, and the leader of the gang Eustace, was expected to undertake royal service when required. In fact, as a consequence of their activities, rough and ready justice and violent redress of wrong became known as Folville's law.

It could well be that in a society which witnessed such violence and longed to express its love of adventure and discontent and also romanticised lawlessness that the ballads of Robin Hood were conceived.

Left. *A fox attired as a bishop preaching to his congregation – a flock of geese. Also a woman hitting a fox for carrying off a goose. An illustration from a medieval manuscript lampooning the church and the people.* (British Library, Roy 10 E IV f 49v).

Top left and top right. *Life in the Middle Ages. Stained glass.*

Top Centre. *Merrymaking. All three from "The Legend of Robyn Hode and Mery Scherewode."*

The mummers of St George

At the end of the 1400's, Robin Hood became a hero of some Mummers' plays which became popular throughout England. From a woodcut in the Pepys Collection, Magdalene College Library, Cambridge.

Robin Hood from the EARLY BALLADS to the Present day

Robin Hood and the May Day and Christmas Festivities

Towards the end of the 1400's, minstrels and their story telling were in decline but Robin Hood remained as popular as ever. He took on a new role and became the star of the silent mummers' plays performed in the open throughout England and Scotland on May Day and at Christmas time. The themes were taken from the Geste and other ballad stories and were no doubt embroidered and embellished as the years passed by. New characters joined the cast including Maid Marian and Friar Tuck for the first time. More important the stories now became mixed up with the tales of Robin Goodfellow, the well known fairy woodland spirit of ancient folklore. Such plays were great local events to which people flocked from miles around. In 1473 a rich knight, Sir John Paston from Norfolk, writing to his brother bemoaned the fact that his servant who played St. George, Robin Hood and the Sheriff of Nottingham had left him.

Robin Hood "games"

By 1500, Robin Hood now joined by Maid Marian moved on from plays to games. They both became popular figures in May and Summer games and often took the role of "King and Queen" of the revels accompanied by the rest of the gang of merry men. For several years the Robin Hood "gatherings" were an important event in the parish of Croscombe in Somerset. In 1480-1, the "Robin Hode" money amounted to 40/4d. (£2.01½). In 1485, "Ric Welles was Roben Hode and presents in for yere past 23/- (£1.15)." The next highest offering was 9/6d. (47½p) for the maidens. At the audit of 1486/7. Robyn Hode presented the Church wardens £3. 6s. 8d. (£3.34), the maidens came next with 20/4d. (£1.01½). The accounts continue over the years until 1526/7 when Robin makes his last appearance with a handsome contribution of £4. 0s. 4d. (4.01½).

Elsewhere, at Kingston-on-Thames, Robin appeared with the Morris Dancers who were becoming an important part of the local scene. In 1515 this versatile character took yet another step. He and his merry men entertained Henry VIII and his court at the May Day celebrations on Shooter's Hill near Greenwich outside London, in a mock ambush. Robin then invited the assembly to the greenwood "to see how the outlaws live."

Robin Hood in Decline

Elizabethan Court Plays

By 1560 the medieval world of the Robin Hood ballads had faded away. The cruel forest laws were no longer in force and sheriffs were not so powerful.

During the 1500's plays became a popular form of entertainment and the theatres grew in stature. From an engraving in Shaw "Dress and Decoration in the Middle Ages."

Archery was no longer a national exercise. The abbeys had been dissolved and the monks had dispersed. Wandering minstrels and their ballads were out of fashion. Robin's fame had temporarily ebbed away. Elizabethan pageantry looked elsewhere for its subject matter. Nevertheless, in several minor plays Robin is featured. He appears as the chief character in two plays by Anthony Munday. The

Left. *Robin Hood and Maid Marian in about 1640. From a contemporary woodcut reproduced from the Roxburghe Ballads (1871-99).* Right. *Engraving from Pierce Egan's "Robin Hood and Little John" (1850).*

first is called "The Downfall of Robert, Earl of Huntingdon." The setting is in the court of King Richard I, who is abroad fighting in the Crusades. Robert is in love with Matilda Fitzwalter. But the king's brother, Prince John, wants her as his mistress. Queen Eleanor, the king's mother, desires Robert as her paramour. True love does not run smoothly. The plot unfolds – Prince John succeeds in outlawing Robert who then assumes the name of Robin Hood. Other well known figures appear including the Sheriff of Nottingham, Eltham, alias Little John, and Skelton, alias Friar Tuck, Scarlet, Scathlock and Much the Miller's Son and a new character – Robin's uncle Gilbert de Hood, Prior of York. In the end the king returns and all is resolved. In the second play, "The Death of Robert, Earl of Huntington," Robert – really Robin Hood – quickly dies leaving his beloved Matilda to the mercy of the lustful Prince John. As Earl of Huntingdon, Robin has moved right up the social ladder from the status of yeoman in the early ballads!

Robin Hood in other guises

In the 1600's and early 1700's Robin had a chequered career. He appears in Ben Johnson's unfinished play "The Sad Shepherd" in 1641 and in other roles such as pageants. In various broadside and garland ballads, Robin is demoted from an Earl to a pleb! But a political ballad appearing in 1727 entitled "Robin Hood and the Duke of Lancaster" equates the Prime Minister Robert Walpole with Robin – a new role! Robin became the subject of several operas and other musical entertainments and old ballad stories were republished.

Robin Hood's Revival

In the late 1700's there was renewed interest in the past and Robin Hood was re-discovered. His principal disciple was Joseph Ritson who published in 1795 his interesting "Robin Hood: A Collection of all the ancient poems, songs and ballads." This was the very first comprehensive collection of such ballads and literary references to be compiled. It included a life of Robin from birth to death claiming to be authentic, but in fact, was based on bogus evidence. Ritson's work had an amazing impact, particularly on children and ran to many editions, inspiring many others to research Robin Hood. It helped to reinstate Robin as a hero in popular imagination. Ritson characterised Robin as "a man who in a barbarous age, and under a complicated tyranny, displayed a spirit of freedom and independence, which has endeared him to the common people whose cause he maintained . . ., and inspite of the malicious endeavours of pitiful monks by whom history has consecrated to the crimes and follies of titled ruffians and sainted idiots, to supress all record of his patriotic exertions and virtuous acts, will render his name immortal." Famous writers took up the Robin Hood theme. For instance, Keats wrote a poem – not one of his best and Sir Walter Scott in 1822 published his famous novel "Ivanhoe." Here he portrays Robin as Locksley a chivalrous hero in the court of King Richard I. In the same year appeared yet another novel – Thomas Peacock's romantic "Maid Marion." Later on, Lord Tennison composed a dramatic poem "The Foresters." Children were entertained with the production of Pierce Egan's splendidly illustrated "Robin Hood and

Little John" in 1840. As the years have passed by, Robin's fame has grown further. More and more authors have applied their pens relating the tales of Robin Hood and his merry men and have gone on to invent new ones.

30

Right. *Robin Hood and the Cinema.*
1. *Figures from Walt Disney's cartoon version.*
2. *Walt Disney's film starring Richard Todd as Robert Fitzooth with Friar Tuck.*
3. *Douglas Fairbanks.*
4. *Douglas Fairbanks this time with Enid Bennett.*
5. *Errol Flynn with Olivia de Havilland.*
6. *From the "Sword of Sherwood Forest."*

Robin Hood on the Screen

This century, films and television have played their part in promoting Robin's image. Several films appeared before the great Hollywood silent black and white classic was launched in 1922 starring Douglas Fairbanks as Robin, Earl of Huntingdon. King Richard is crusading in the Holyland. Prince John is the villain and Maid Marion, no doubt representing the emancipated woman, plays a dominant role.

Warner Brother's lavish epic production of "Robin Hood" costing $2,000,000 appeared in technicolour and sound in 1938. Errol Flynn as the swash buckling hero Robin, starred with eye-flashing Olivia de Havilland of course as Maid Marion.

In 1952, Walt Disney took up the challenge. His "Story of Robin Hood and his merry men" cost even more than the Warner Brother's epic. Richard Todd played Robert Fitzooth, a forester, alias Robin Hood and Joan Price as Maid Marion. The merry men are also there. The "Sword of Sherwood Forest'" was screened in 1961 starring Richard Greene. Walt Disney was back again in 1973 with his cartoon version with Robin as a fox and Maid Marion as a super vixen. In 1975, "Robin and Marion" was filmed on location, not in Sherwood Forest, but in Spain. The famous couple in the guise Sean Connery and Audrey Hepburn live happily on into middle age after all their adventures. Over the years, television has raised Robin to stardom. He has moved into the world of science fiction and conquering outer space and has been linked up with the stars in "Star Trek." Where will he move next?

Robin Hood PLACE NAMES

Throughout Britain and far off Australia and the United States, Robin is remembered through hundreds of place, street and pub names. The ballads originally spread his fame. Even in 1319, there was a cross near Hathersage in Derbyshire which might possibly be linked with him. The charters of Monk Bretton Priory in Yorkshire compiled in 1422 link sites in the Barnsdale area with the outlaw and the stories in the Geste. Many place names must have been in existence long before they were recorded in ink. Others have vanished. Some have even changed their meaning over the centuries. All over Britain there are wells, caves, chairs, leaps, rocks, beds, tables and even graves. No one else has been so remembered. In Derbyshire, two pinnacles of stone about forty feet apart are known as Robin Hood's stride – presumably, Robin would have won any Olympic long jump with yards to spare! In Nottinghamshire particularly he lives on together with his merrymen and Maid Marian – pubs, inns and restaurants called after them abound.

32

1. *Robin Hood's Bay, near Whitby, Yorkshire.*   2. *Robin Hood's Stride, near Elton, Derbyshire.*   3. *Carved fireplace at Thoresby Hall, near Ollerton, Nottinghamshire depicting a Sherwood forest scene supported by statues of the outlaws.*
4. *Robin Hood pub at Lambley, Nottinghamshire.*   5. *St. Mary's Church, Nottinghamshire where according to the Geste Robin Hood prayed.*   6. *Creswell Crags, near Worksop, Nottinghamshire, the biggest cave is named after Robin Hood.*

NORTHUMBERLAND

A bog near Chillingham and a rock near Dunstanburgh.

CUMBRIA

A hill near Shap. A grave near Crosby Ravensworth Fell. An island and a wood near Kendal. A field called Robin Hood's Buttes near Brampton and a chair at Ennerdale Water.

LANCASHIRE

A hamlet near Wrightington. A ridge on Blackstone Edge called Robin Hood's Bed. A cross near Mawdsley, and a house near Wigan.

CHESHIRE

A field near Runcorn.

DERBYSHIRE

A hamlet near Baslow. A cave, a croft, a cross, a moss (or bog), a stone known as Robin Hood's Stoop, a well, and a spring, all near Hathersage. A chair near Hope Dale. Two stone pillars called Robin Hood's Picking Rods near Ludworth. Two broken rocks on a hilltop known as Robin Hood's stride near Elton. A table and a leap near Chatsworth. Little John's Grave and Well at Hathersage.

HEREFORD & WORCESTER

A burial mound near Church Stretton called Robin Hood's Butts. Two round-topped hills near Weobley.

GLOUCESTERSHIRE

A hill near Gloucester.

SOMERSET

Two separate groups of long barrows near Taunton, both known as Robin Hood's Butts.

WARWICKSHIRE

A farm near Birmingham. Loxley near Stratford-on-Avon reputed by some to be Robin Hood's birth place.

WILTSHIRE

A burial mound called Robin Hood's Ball at Netheravon and an earthwork known as Robin Hood's Bower near Warminster.

BERKSHIRE

A farm near Reading and an earthwork called Robin Hood's Arbour in Maidenhead. Little John's Farm near Reading.

NORTH, WEST & SOUTH YORKSHIRE

A tower on the city walls at York. A hamlet near Catterick Bridge. A bay near Whitby. Several burial mounds or earthwords all called Robin Hood's Butts, near Danby, near Romaldkirk and at Robin Hood's Bay. A hollow called Robin Hood's Howl near Kirkbymoorside. A tower at Richmond Castle. A well at Wensley. A small field at Whitby, adjacent to Little John's Close. A village near Leeds. A grave at Kirklees. A hill and a house near Almondbury. A hill at Outwood. A park near Fountains Abbey. A rocking-stone on Midgley Moor and a stone near Halifax, both called Robin Hood's Penny Stone. A stone at Silsden. Six different wells near Doncaster, near Threshfield, near Halton Gill, near Fountains Abbey, near Ecclesfield and near Haworth. A wood near Fountains Abbey.

Barnsdale, Barnsdale Bar, Sayles, Wentbridge all mentioned in the Geste, north of Doncaster. Loxley west of Sheffield is reputed by some to have been Robin Hood's birth place.

LONDON

A lane and a yard and also several courts now lost. In Richmond Park a walk, a gate and a farm. Near Kingston-on-Thames a hamlet, and a way.

SURREY

Two hills near Godalming once called Robin Hood's Butts.

ESSEX

A hamlet near Finchingfield, and a farm close by.

NOTTINGHAMSHIRE

Three caves, one near Walesby, another near Mansfield and the other at Creswell Crags. A farm near Nottingham. A burial mound near Oxton called Robin Hood Hill. Robin Hood's Hills south of Mansfield associated with his cave and his chair. A field named Robin Hood's Meadow at Perlethorpe. A cave cut into the rocks near Papplewick called Robin Hood's Stable. A well near Greasley, Fountaindale and Friar Tuck's Well near Mansfield by tradition both linked with the worthy friar. Edwinstowe church by tradition the scene of the marriage between Robin Hood and Maid Marian. At Papplewick Church Allan A Dale is reputed to have married. Sherwood Forest once covered most of the county. In Nottingham the Castle and St. Mary's Church are named in the ballad stories. Also Maid Marian Way and Robin Hood's Acre, Close and Well. Numerous statues, pubs, restaurants and garages throughout the county linked with Robin and the merry men.

NORFOLK

Rocks near Sheringham called Robin's Friend.

LEICESTERSHIRE

In Leicester Little John's Stone, and in Charnwood Forest a hill named Little John.

NORTHAMPTONSHIRE

Two stones near Peterborough called Robin Hood and Little John.

Statue of Robin Hood at Nottingham Castle.

PLACES ASSOCIATED WITH THE ROBIN HOOD LEGENDS